STEP FIVE
And the Truth Will Set You Free

First published March, 1983.

Copyright © 1983 by Hazelden Foundation
All rights reserved.
No part of this booklet may be reproduced
without the written permission of the publisher.
ISBN: 0-89486-165-4

Printed in the United States of America.

The following is an adaptation of one of the Twelve Steps in the program of Overeaters Anonymous. It is one person's interpretation and does not speak for the O.A. organization.

Turning point

"We must be entirely honest with somebody if we expect to live long or happily in this world."* Many of us would add: and if we expect to recover from compulsive overeating and maintain long-term abstinence and serenity, the same rule applies.

Step Five can be a turning point for those of us who have felt alienated from a Higher Power, ourselves, and other people. Candidly telling another person everything in our Fourth Step inventory fosters a deep sense of healing and belonging. Maybe we do not fully know ourselves. Nor can we entirely accept ourselves until we put our thoughts and feelings into words and share our self-discovery with someone else.

"Until we actually sit down and talk about what we have so long hidden, our willingness to clean house is still largely theoretical. When we are honest with another person, it confirms that we have been honest with ourselves and with God."**

The object of Steps Four and Five is not to become martyrs nor to put ourselves down in a masochistic way. Rather, the purpose is to become aware of the ways in which we sabotage our ability to change.

***Alcoholics Anonymous,** published by A.A. World Services, New York, NY, p. 73. Available through Hazelden Educational Materials.

Twelve Steps and Twelve Traditions, published by A.A. World Services, New York, NY, p. 61. Available through Hazelden Educational Materials.

Fear and anxiety result from trying to cover up our defects and our liabilities. We live with an ever-present threat of exposure. But when we are completely honest with a sympathetic friend or counselor, when we carefully examine the problem areas of our behavior and balance our liabilities against our current assets or those we are trying to develop, we no longer have anything to hide. What a relief! Taking responsibility, out loud, for what we have done and left undone is the first step toward changing what we don't like about ourselves.

For many of us, sharing our inventory with someone we respect and trust, and feeling understood and accepted by that person is the beginning of what the program describes as a spiritual awakening. The experience of forgiveness and reconciliation marks a turning point in our lives.

Admitting to God and ourselves

Before we found the program, some of us spent a good part of our lives trying to run away from our Higher Power as well as from our inner selves. Much of our difficulty with the idea of a Higher Power is caused by pride. For years we have been intent on proving how well we could get along on our own, without God as we understand Him, and without listening to an inner voice. It takes humility to admit, "Okay, H.P., I've really made a mess of things. I've flunked out of school because I wasn't willing to work, and I've damaged my body by habitual self-indulgence." Or, "I see that my petty resentment and jealousy have been a major cause of the strained relationship between my brother and me. I've been a real pain." Humility is part of recovery.

So the first thing that Step Five suggests we do is admit to God and to ourselves just where we have gone off the track. You may be asking, "Isn't that a little silly? I'm not going to be telling my Higher Power or myself anything we don't already know."

True. But if you have thoroughly worked the preceding Steps, you are developing a new, more meaningful relationship with the God of your understanding. And you are learning to be more honest with yourself. You have learned that others have recovered through trust in a Higher Power and an honest effort to be open to inner guidance from that Higher Power.

Admitting to God the exact nature of our wrongs puts us in an immediate relationship with Him. It is a right relationship, because we are acknowledging that we haven't done all that well on our own and that we need help. Admitting our mistakes usually includes feelings of regret and remorse. That's painful. But unless we are willing to take responsibility for our actions, we will continue to run away from reality. When we accept the truth—both its pleasant and unpleasant aspects—we can experience the acceptance and forgiveness of a Higher Power. Then we can forgive and accept ourselves.

Seeing who we really are, our assets and our liabilities, liberates us from the game of trying to fool ourselves. We may have made a considerable effort to ignore and forget behavior that has embarrassed us and made us ashamed. Perhaps we have tended to blame anyone and everyone else for our problems, blinding ourselves to our own responsibility for them. In this program, we learn that we cannot change other people. We are not responsible for what they do. We are, however, responsible for what we do and how we *react* to what others do. Through the help of a Higher Power, we can change our own behavior.

 Seeking another human being

"Somehow, being alone with God doesn't seem as embarrassing as facing up to another person."*

Do you have the feeling that you have always been different from "normal" people? ...That if others knew you as you really are, they would quickly reject you? Does being around people seem to require an exhaustive effort for you to be acceptable in their eyes? How much energy do you spend "hiding" from those around you? Do you have a secret life?

Compulsive overeating is a lonely disease. In our overeating careers all of us have done things for which we're ashamed, whether these actions were related or unrelated to food. We've tried to cover up traces of binges and other negative behaviors so no one would know. The more we cover up, the more isolated we become.

What the OA program demands of us is rigorous honesty, and that is difficult if not impossible to achieve alone. We need the healing that comes from opening the dark corner of ourselves to another human being. Step Five requires courage, sometimes more than we think we have, until we

*Twelve Steps and Twelve Traditions, published by A.A. World Services, New York, NY, p. 61. Available through Hazelden Educational Materials.

remember that a Power greater than ourselves is leading and supporting us. That makes all the difference. We are not doing this alone. Help is available for the asking. Wanting to get well gives us courage.

How do you choose the person with whom to share your Fifth Step? The most important criteria are that the person be someone with whom you are comfortable, who will understand what you are doing in Step Five, and who can be trusted to protect your anonymity. He or she may be a member of the clergy, a counselor, your sponsor or someone else in the program, a friend, or even a complete stranger. What counts is that another human being is receiving you just as you are, the good and the bad.

If you haven't already completed your inventory, one way to motivate yourself is to make a definite appointment with the person you choose for Step Five. You may be reluctant to call someone and request help. Ask yourself if your reluctance is because you are shy or because you are proud. If being completely honest with God and ourselves requires humility, revealing ourselves to another person requires even more. When we decide we cannot afford to be too proud to ask for help, we are heading for recovery.

"Experience has taught us we cannot live alone with our pressing problems and the character defects which cause or aggravate them. If Step Four has revealed in stark relief those experiences we'd rather not remember, then the need to quit living by ourselves with those tormenting ghosts of yesterday gets more urgent than ever. We have to talk to somebody about them."*

***Twelve Steps and Twelve Traditions,** published by A.A. World Services, New York, NY, p. 56. Available through Hazelden Educational Materials.

Exactly the way it is

"I can't tell anyone that I stole money out of my mother's purse to buy candy when I was a child.....That I slept with my boss in order to get a promotion.....That I can't be in the same room with my son for 15 minutes without yelling at him, and that he's been arrested three times.....That I hide boxes of junk food on my closet shelf.....That the reason I took a job in another city and relocated my family was to get away from all the lies I had told.....That the reason I didn't go to an important social function last week was because none of my clothes fit, and I was too gorged to move."

If you have chosen a sympathetic, understanding person who has had some experience with life and with people, it is unlikely that anything you say will come as an overwhelming shock to him or her. Probably your confidant will be honored to share something which is so important to you. Most likely the person will react to your sincerity and honesty with a great deal of respect and a genuine desire to help.

How would you feel if someone asked a similar favor of you? Do you think you are head and shoulders above everyone else in your willingness to be helpful? If you have chosen to share your inventory with another member of the program, the experience will undoubtedly be as beneficial to him or her as it is to you. That's the way this program works—we can't keep it unless we give it away.

Holding back what you feel is too embarrassing to reveal will only detract from the cleansing process and the feeling of peace which eventually you want to experience. If you deal only in vague generalities such as, "I've always been afraid," or "I get mad easily," you are depriving yourself of the exact incidents that have made you feel guilty. Be specific. You may not want to share some of your personal problems with family members and others close to you. But here you are with an understanding listener, one you trust to protect your anonymity. Now is your chance. You are not trying to impress the other person; you are working for recovery.

You may wish to read your inventory just as you have written it, or you may want to expand and fill in details. If your listener is familiar with the program, he or she might suggest beginning the session with a short prayer. Those who have taken the Fourth and Fifth Steps, themselves, perhaps will want to share parts of their own inventories or relate to your experience with some of theirs. Whatever happens, chances are you will feel much better when you leave the session than when you came. Remember, the more specific and exact you are, the more freedom you will know when you have "given away" your inventory.

Like the rest of the program, the Fifth Step works. The psychological and spiritual value of confession has been demonstrated for centuries. In the Twelve Step programs, we are taking advantage of a proven method of enhancing emotional health and spiritual well-being. More than that, the ability to be honest with ourselves, God and our fellow human beings has become crucially important for those of us who seek recovery from compulsive overeating.

Often we discover that what had seemed so shameful in our own minds is not that grim when exposed to the light of day and a "sympathetic other." Mistakes from the past are particularly apt to get blown out of proportion simply because we have kept them to ourselves. No matter what we have or have not done, the past is over and can be forgiven. By telling our story like it is, we can lay to rest "those tormenting ghosts of yesterday."*

Join the human race

Part of the necessary ego-reduction we must go through in order to recover from our illness has to do with accepting the fact that we are human and make mistakes. Since a compulsive overeater is often a perfectionist, such acceptance is not easy. Trying to do things perfectly can apply to anything from a food plan, to writing a report, to cleaning a house. The harder we try, the more anxiety we experience. When we do make an error, we use that as an excuse to hate ourselves and to stop trying. How is a compulsive overeater tempted to relieve anxiety and self-hate? By overeating, of course.

In Step Five, we say to our Higher Power, ourselves and another person, "All right. I'm not perfect. And here is some of the evidence." We become willing to present ourselves as we are without hiding the blemishes. Instead of trying to maintain an image of superiority, we analyze our weaknesses so we can make constructive changes. Usually our listener can help us see that our image of superiority was unnecessary in the first place, and it only got in our way. No one can avoid making mistakes. So why be miserable attempting to do the impossible?

*Ibid.

Of course you're not perfect. Who is? Why not join the human race, and together let's see what we can do about accepting ourselves as we are right now. That is where we start. Any progress which is made has to begin with what we are today.

Learning to trust

With Step Five we begin to remove the walls we have created between ourselves and other people. It has been said that we can only know as much of ourselves as we are willing to reveal to someone else. But in order to be willing to reveal ourselves, we need to trust the other person. If in the past you have been afraid that people would let you down, you may have decided to "go it alone." How well has that worked?

Experience has demonstrated that until we come out of the self-imposed emotional isolation which often goes along with compulsive overeating, we do not recover. It is not only our eating habits which have gone awry; our interpersonal relationships often leave us unfulfilled and empty. Coming to this program is an admission that we are sick and tired of trying to go it alone. However frightening it may be to trust someone else to help us, it is worse to continue down the path of solitary self-destruction. Through the program, we are led to people we *can* trust and to friends who do not let us down.

For a variety of reasons, many of us have become very good at hiding from other people. (A favorite hiding place for a compulsive overeater is, of course, the refrigerator.) Coming out of hiding goes hand in hand with developing a sense of trust. One is not possible without the other. We do not learn to trust a Higher Power, ourselves and other people until we stop hiding, and we only stop hiding as we develop enough confidence to reveal who we really are. It happens little by little. Trusting another person with our inner selves does not stop with the Fifth Step; it is an ongoing process throughout our recovery.

We come to this program and hear other people talk who have had experiences similar to ours. We can relate to what they say, and we can relate to them as fellow compulsive overeaters and fellow human beings. We feel at home. We begin to share our own experiences, and find that people don't laugh or think we're crazy. They understand. It feels good to be able to talk about what we tried to hide, and it helps to get feedback from empathetic friends.

So we begin to reach out, to reveal a little more about ourselves, to trust in an ever-widening circle of people. After all, what have we got to lose? O.A. says if we don't like the program, our misery will be cheerfully refunded. How can we withhold trust from those who have been through the same sort of hell that we have, and who sincerely want to help? Sharing our inventories is a giant step toward learning to trust other people. We gain a new sense of belonging and relatedness. We're less alone. The world becomes less fearful.

Communicating

After fully revealing yourself to another person in Step Five, you will find more freedom to be honest and open in other relationships, too. The dark secrets are off your chest. You don't have to hide and cover up any more. Self-respect soars with the feeling of having nothing to conceal.

The desire to communicate is one of our deepest cravings. As children we are relatively candid and spontaneous in the way we express ourselves, and we talk about what is important to us. As we grow older, we become more wary of expressing how we really feel. We may stop telling it like it is. Instead, we tell the people we love what we think they want to hear. We become afraid to say things that might upset an important relationship.

In our interaction with other people, we may build up defenses so no one will be able to penetrate the image we are attempting to project. Defending an image is solitary business. It leads to superficial conversation which fails to satisfy our need to relate to others on a meaningful level. If we are trying to present an image of how we think we should be—cool, sophisticated, tough, smart, gracious, whatever— we are relating in an artificial way. The image isn't real. The communication doesn't satisfy.

Lacking the warmth of genuine interaction with the important people in our lives, those of us who are compulsive overeaters turn to food to fill the emptiness. As our defenses build, pride prevents us from reaching out to other people. "I don't need anyone. I can be self-sufficient. I can take care of myself." We pretend that everything is fine—all we need to do is lose a few pounds. What problems we have are someone else's fault. We will not display any hint of weakness, because that would threaten the image we have carefully worked to create.

If we only tell people the good things, we are trying to live a lie. Worst of all, we cut ourselves off from feedback and from outside help to deal with life's gut-level difficulties.

There is the possibility of going to the other extreme and pouring out never-ending tales of woe. That doesn't make for satisfying communication either. Even though we will probably do most of the talking in our Fifth Step, we also will listen carefully to our listener's reaction.

Going over our inventory and our story with someone else gives us the benefit of a fresh perspective and another person's experience. We don't have to keep trying to sort out the problems alone. An honest response to what we have to share increases our self-knowledge and confidence. Even an attitude of quiet listening conveys understanding and acceptance to us. Through Step Five we become more open to the possibility of genuine communication. We learn from the insights of others, and our hunger for genuine communication is satisfied.

 Toward recovery

Our journey toward recovery continues. When we share our inventory and those experiences and feelings which have troubled us most, we come out of isolation. We make a breakthrough toward improved relationships with other people. These relationships will eventually provide us with the kind of emotional nourishment that food never did and never will. Cleansing and healing take place, opening the way for further emotional and spiritual growth.

Many who have taken Step Five report that they experience the love, acceptance and forgiveness of a Higher Power in a tangible way. As so often happens with the program, this gift from a Higher Power is often mediated through another person. When we feel the love and acceptance of another human being who knows "the worst" about us, simultaneously we can feel the forgiveness of our Higher Power. This sets us free to be who we are.

Sometimes the experience is described as one of rebirth. It is as though the past has been wiped clean and laid to rest, making possible a new beginning. We get rid of some of the emotional roadblocks—especially guilt and fear. Then we are able to move on. This may mean finally having the courage to go back to school, to look for a new job, to extricate ourselves from damaging relationships, to make positive commitments. The healing that comes with this Step can give us a fresh perspective on how we want to spend the rest of our lives, one day at a time.

Most important, we are continuing to grow spiritually. A Higher Power is here with us when we acknowledge our need for Him. We admit our weaknesses and our failures, and we are given strength to try again, this time with new insight and new faith. The Fifth Step is not something we do once and for all. It's an ongoing process. As we develop and change, we will probably want to make periodic inventories to evaluate our progress. Each time we share them, we get rid of more debris and make new, positive discoveries.

As we move through the Steps toward recovery, we are moving into freedom. Freedom from food abuse and the self-destructive habit of overeating is what we were desperately seeking when we came to this program. But we find more. We find forgiveness and love. We find new possibilities for handling difficult situations constructively.

There may be an actual physical sensation of relief and lightness after taking Step Five. There also will be progress toward the emotional freedom and self-knowledge that makes it possible to maintain abstinence. With the Fifth Step we take another stride toward closer relationships with our fellow human beings and toward the spiritual freedom that comes from daily surrender to a Power greater than ourselves.